Work from Lunch Ideas

Find the Perfect Balance of Nutrition and Taste

BY - Stephanie Sharp

Copyright © 2020 by Stephanie Sharp

License Notes

Copyright 2020 by Stephanie Sharp All rights reserved.

No part of this Book may be transmitted or reproduced into any format for any means without the proper permission of the Author. This includes electronic or mechanical methods, photocopying or printing.

The Reader assumes all risk when following any of the guidelines or ideas written as they are purely suggestion and for informational purposes. The Author has taken every precaution to ensure accuracy of the work but bears no responsibility if damages occur due to a misinterpretation of suggestions.

wwwwwwwwwwwwwwwwwwwwwwwwww

My deepest thanks for buying my book! Now that you have made this investment in time and money, you are now eligible for free e-books on a weekly basis! Once you subscribe by filling in the box below with your email address, you will start to receive free and discounted book offers for unique and informative books. There is nothing more to do! A reminder email will be sent to you a few days before the promotion expires so you will never have to worry about missing out on this amazing deal. Enter your email address below to get started. Thanks again for your purchase!

Just visit the link or scan QR-code to get started!

https://stephanie-sharp.subscribemenow.com

Table of Contents

Introduction 8

Recipes 10

    Whole Bread Turkey Sandwich with fruits 11

    Baked Chicken Breasts with Fruits and Nuts 14

    Kale Apple Cheery Yogurt Salad 17

    Salmon with Baby Potatoes Broccoli Green Beans 19

    Egg Ramen Fry 22

    Brown Tortilla Wrap with Apples 25

    Quinoa with Shrimp and Tomato Salsa 27

    Kidney Beans with Mango, Avocado and veggies 30

    Watermelon Olive Cherry Tomato Cucumber Salad 32

    Cucumber Tomato Brazil nut Salad 34

    Baked Beef with Fresh Veggies 36

    Beetroot Arugula Olive Pasta Salad 39

Green Salad with Grilled Chicken 41

Mexican Style Chicken Avocado Corn Tomato Salad . 44

Honey Glazed Chicken Pan Fry with Simple Salad...... 47

Boiled Pasta with Duck and Veggies 50

Roasted Sweet Potato Kale and Chickpeas 53

Cauliflower Risotto with Fried Scallops 56

Sesame Chicken with Butter tossed Broccoli and Sticky Rice... 59

Chicken Cheesy Sub Sandwich...................................... 62

Simple Vegan Sandwich 64

Quinoa Salmon Veggie Salad 66

Croquette Wrap 69

Brown Rice with Yogurt Chicken.................................. 72

Pan Fried Crispy Cod with Veggies.............................. 75

Turkey Avocado Lettuce Goat Cheese Salad................ 78

Minced Chicken Red Beans Tomato Curry with Cabbage and Avocado.. 81

Chickpea Croutons Avocado Baby Cabbage Salad 84

Quinoa 87

Fish with Green Beans Cherry Tomato and Olives 90

Conclusion 93

About the Author 94

Author's Afterthoughts.. 95

Introduction

Working from home is not too different when you go to your office and work there. You still need to meet your deadlines when you work from home. You still have to do the same amount of work. You need to keep yourself focused all the time. So, to achieve productivity during your office hours at home, you have to eat good food. Lunch that caters to providing energy and restoring your lethargy. Fried and greasy food makes you lethargic. You cannot take a nap after your lunch because you are working from home.

So, we have compiled 30 working from home lunch recipes that are very healthy and quick to make. You will find a lot of salad recipes in the book. It is because salad is easy to prepare and it usually contains a lot of greens, which is very good for our body. There are many sandwich recipes too. It is another quick lunch idea and some people enjoy eating hand food during work hours. You will also find some fancy dishes. Those are there to give you treat during your office hours occasionally.

Recipes

Whole Bread Turkey Sandwich with fruits

Working from home does not mean you relax and invest hours in your eating. It should be just as compact and healthy as it is when you get physically to work. This is a perfect combination of nutrition and convenient lunch food.

Serving Size: 1

Cooking Time: 5 Minutes

Ingredients:

- 2 whole wheat bread slices
- 2 thin slices of turkey
- 1 tsp olive oil
- Salt and pepper to taste
- 2 lettuce leaves
- 1 thin cheese slice
- 1 tbsp ketchup
- 4 strawberries, diced
- 1 kiwi, diced
- 1/3 cup blueberries
- 1/3 cup grapes

Instructions:

In a pan add the oil and add the turkey slices.

Sprinkle some salt, pepper and cook for 2 minutes on each side.

Add the ketchup on the bread slice. Add a piece of lettuce leaf, turkey slice following by a cheese slice.

Add another turkey slice and then the remaining lettuce leaf.

Top with another bread slice.

Toss the fruits together and enjoy.

Baked Chicken Breasts with Fruits and Nuts

A lunch during your working hours should be not too filling that you want to take a nap. But it still should be tasty and easy to make. This lunch dish is fairly easy and quick to prepare.

Serving Size: 1

Cooking Time: 20 Minutes

Ingredients:

- 1 ripe avocado
- 4 cherry tomatoes
- 2 baby cucumbers
- 1 tsp sesame seeds
- Salt to taste
- Black pepper to taste
- 2 chicken breasts
- 1 tsp honey
- 1 tbsp oil
- 1 tsp garlic powder
- 2 tbsp walnuts
- 2 tbsp brazil nuts

Instructions:

Cut the avocado in half and sprinkle some sesame seeds, salt and pepper on top.

Cut the cucumbers into thick slices. Add them in a container.

For the chicken coat it in salt, garlic powder, honey, pepper and oil.

Add to a baking tray and bake for 20 minutes.

Let it rest for some time and then cut it into thick slices.

Combine the chicken with the fruits and nuts and enjoy.

Kale Apple Cheery Yogurt Salad

There is nothing better than a good fruit salad mixed with yogurt. It takes less than 10 minutes to prepare and there is no hassle of cooking!

Serving Size: 1

Ingredients:

- 2 apples, cubed
- 1 cup kale, chopped
- 1 cup yogurt
- 1 tbsp honey
- 1 pinch of sea salt
- 1 pinch of pepper
- 6 cherries, thinly sliced

Instructions:

In a bowl or box, combine the apples, kale, and cherries.

Add the yogurt and mix well.

Add the salt, pepper, and honey. Coat well and serve cold.

Salmon with Baby Potatoes Broccoli Green Beans

When you are working for a long hour, you need protein to remain calm and get your brain functioning properly. This lunch recipe contains many veggies to go with it too.

Serving Size: 1

Cooking Time: 20 Minutes

Ingredients:

- 1 salmon fillet, boneless, skinless
- 1/3 cup broccoli florets, diced
- 6 green beans
- 1 carrot, peeled, sliced
- 6 baby potatoes
- Salt and pepper to taste
- 1 tbsp apple cider vinegar
- 2 tbsp butter
- ¼ tsp rosemary
- 1 tsp garlic powder
- ½ tsp paprika

Instructions:

Marinate the fish with garlic powder, salt, paprika and rosemary. Let it sit for 10 minutes.

In a pan melt half the butter.

Add the salmon and fry for 3 minutes on each side.

Transfer to your plate.

In the same pan add the rest of the butter.

Toss the baby potatoes in low flame for 5 minutes. Sprinkle some salt, pepper and cook for 2 minutes.

Add the carrots, green beans, and broccoli.

Add the apple cider vinegar and some more salt and pepper.

Toss for 5 minutes. Serve with the fish.

Egg Ramen Fry

Stir fried ramen is perhaps one of the most consumed Asian dish out there. It is for the simple reason of quick prep. It takes less than 15 minutes to make it. Try this recipe and see how your lunch hours become quick and delicious.

Serving Size: 1

Cooking Time: 15 Minutes

Ingredients:

- 2 eggs
- 1 packet ramen, about 250 g
- ¼ cup scallion, chopped
- Salt and pepper to taste
- 2 tbsp tomato sauce
- 2 onion, chopped
- 2 tbsp oil
- 1 tsp sesame seeds
- ¼ cup grated cheese

Instructions:

Boil the ramen with salted water. It should take about 6 minutes.

Drain it and pour cold water on top.

in another pot boil one egg for 6 minutes. Drain and let it cool down. Remove the shell once it cools down and cut it in half. Set aside.

In a wok, heat the oil and scramble the egg. Add some salt and pepper.

Add the onion and toss for 2 minutes.

Add the boiled ramen, tomato sauce, sesame seeds, cheese and cook for 3 minutes.

Add the scallions on top and the boiled egg on top before serving.

Brown Tortilla Wrap with Apples

Wraps are great options for lunch during work because it is easy to eat in a hurry. It is also not too difficult to make either. I have added apple slices on the side to balance the nutrition value.

Serving Size: 1

Cooking Time: 30 Minutes

Ingredients:

- 1 brown tortilla
- 1 cup left-over chicken meat
- ½ cup kale, chopped
- 1 red onion, sliced
- 1 tbsp mayo
- 1 apple, cut into wedges

Instructions:

In a pan add the tortilla and fry it for 1 minute per side.

Transfer to a plate. Spread the mayo.

Add the chicken meat, onion slices, kale and roll the tortilla tightly.

Cut it into half. Enjoy. Add the apples on the side of the plate before serving.

Quinoa with Shrimp and Tomato Salsa

If you love eating grains in general then your lunch would be incomplete without any grains. This is a simple spicy quinoa recipe with pan fried shrimps and a killer salsa to go with it.

Serving Size: 1

Cooking Time: 15 Minutes

Ingredients:

- 2 tomatoes, chopped
- 1 red onion, sliced
- 1 tsp chopped coriander
- Salt and pepper to taste
- 1 tsp lemon juice
- 1 cup shrimp, peeled, deveined
- 1 cup quinoa
- 1 tsp paprika
- 1 tbsp oil
- 1 tbsp butter
- ¼ tsp dried oregano
- 1 tbsp honey
- 1 tbsp BBQ sauce

Instructions:

Combine the honey, BBQ sauce and toss the shrimp in it.

In a pan add the butter and fry the shrimps for 2 minutes on each side.

For the quinoa, in a pan add the oil. Add the quinoa with ½ cup of water.

Add oregano, paprika, salt and pepper. Cover and cook for 10 minutes.

Fluff it using a fork and serve hot.

For the salsa, combine the tomato, onion, salt, pepper, coriander and lemon juice. Toss well and serve.

Kidney Beans with Mango, Avocado and veggies

Have you ever tried eating kidney beans with mangoes or avocado before? To add more crunch and texture, there is red chili, cherry tomatoes and scallions.

Serving Size: 1

Ingredients:

- 1 cup boiled kidney beans
- 1 mango, cut into cubes
- 1 avocado, cut into cubes
- 1 tsp chopped coriander leaves
- Salt and pepper to taste
- 1 tbsp apple cider vinegar
- ½ cup cherry tomatoes cut in half
- 2 tbsp scallions, chopped
- 1 red chili, chopped

Instructions:

In a large bowl combine the veggies and fruits.

Add the kidney beans and toss gently.

Add the red chili, coriander leaves, salt, pepper, scallions, apple cider vinegar and toss again.

Serve.

Watermelon Olive Cherry Tomato Cucumber Salad

When you are too busy doing your work at home, this is one of the best way to boast your energy without investing much time behind it. Add your favorite juice on the side and enjoy.

Serving Size: 1

Ingredients:

- 2 baby cucumbers, chopped
- 4 red cherry tomatoes cut in half
- 2 yellow cherry tomatoes cut in half
- 4 black olives, sliced
- 1 cup chopped watermelon
- 1 tbsp honey
- 1 pinch of sea salt

Instructions:

In a bowl, combine the cherry tomatoes with cucumber.

Add the olives, watermelon, and cucumber.

Add the honey and salt and toss gently.

Cucumber Tomato Brazil nut Salad

If you are into super healthy food, then this refreshing salad recipe is for you. The brazil nuts add a lot of crunch and flavor to this salad.

Serving Size: 1

Ingredients:

- 2 cucumber, diced
- 2 tomatoes, chopped
- 2 tbsp brazil nuts, toasted
- 1 red onion, chopped
- Salt and pepper to taste
- 1 tsp honey
- 1 tsp apple cider vinegar

Instructions:

Combine the honey, apple cider vinegar, salt, and pepper. Mix well.

In a bowl combine the tomato, cucumber and onion.

Mix well and add the nuts and the dressing.

Toss again and serve.

Baked Beef with Fresh Veggies

If you love beef, you will love this simple and healthy beef dish that takes no extra preparation. The veggies can be according to your choice. You do not need any extra dressing for the veggies.

Serving Size: 1

Cooking Time: 30 Minutes

Ingredients:

- 1 beef steak
- 1 tsp BBQ sauce
- Salt and black pepper to taste
- ¼ tsp garlic powder
- ½ tsp dried oregano
- 1 baby cucumber, cubed
- 1 yellow bell pepper, chopped
- 1 tomato, chopped

Instructions:

Marinate the beef with BBQ sauce, salt, pepper, garlic powder and oregano.

Let it sit for 30 minutes.

In a baking tray, add an aluminum foil.

Add the beef steak. Bake for 15 minutes with 350 degrees F.

Flip the steak and bake for 5 minutes. Let it rest for 10 minutes. Cut it into four separate pieces. It will be easier to eat during your lunch hour.

Add the veggies together and sprinkle some salt and pepper.

Serve the steak with the veggies.

Beetroot Arugula Olive Pasta Salad

Pasta is one of the easiest dishes to make and pasta salad when tossed with your favorite veggies tastes quite good. It takes only 10 minutes to cook this.

Serving Size: 1

Cooking Time: 10 Minutes

Ingredients:

- 2 baby beetroots cut in half
- 4 cherry tomatoes cut in half
- 1 cup arugula, chopped
- 1 tbsp chopped coriander leaves
- Salt and black pepper to taste
- 1 white onion, chopped
- 2 tbsp mayo
- 1 tsp ketchup
- 6 green olives, halved
- 1 green chili, chopped

Instructions:

In a pot boil the pasta for 8 minutes.

Drain and place in a bowl.

Add the olives, beetroot, onion, green chili, coriander, arugula and cherry tomatoes.

Add the mayo, salt, pepper and ketchup.

Mix well. Serve in room temperature or cold.

Green Salad with Grilled Chicken

This dish may look fancy but it takes very little effort on your end. The grilled chicken complements the greens in the salad properly.

Serving Size: 1

Cooking Time: 10 Minutes

Ingredients:

- 1 chicken breast
- ½ tsp garlic powder
- ½ tsp lemon juice
- Salt and black pepper to taste
- ¼ tsp rosemary
- 1 cup collar leaves, chopped
- ¼ cup brussels sprouts, halved
- 3 cherry tomatoes, chopped
- 2 baby onion, diced
- 2 tbsp olive oil
- 1 tbsp apple cider vinegar

Instructions:

Marinate the chicken breast with garlic powder, lemon juice, rosemary, salt and pepper.

In a grilling pan, add 1 tbsp olive oil. Add the chicken breast and grill for 5 minutes on each side.

Let it rest for 10 minutes. Cut into thick slices.

In a bowl combine all the veggies.

Add salt, pepper, apple cider vinegar and olive oil. Toss well and serve with chicken pieces on the side.

Mexican Style Chicken Avocado Corn Tomato Salad

Mexican food uses a lot of corn and tomatoes in there cooking. This salad also contains avocado which is a super-food. The tiny piece of chicken adds a lot of flavors in the salad.

Serving Size: 1

Cooking Time: 10 Minutes

Ingredients:

- 1 semi ripe avocado, cubed
- 1 chicken breast
- Salt and pepper to taste
- 1 cup corn kernels
- 2 tomatoes, chopped
- ½ cup chopped cabbage
- 1 tsp olive oil
- 2 lettuce leaves, chopped
- 2 tbsp mayo
- 1 tbsp lemon juice
- 1/3 tsp rosemary
- 1/3 tsp garlic powder

Instructions:

Coat the chicken with rosemary, garlic powder, salt and pepper.

In a pan add the oil and fry the chicken breast for 4 minutes per side.

Let it cool down, chop it finely.

In a bowl add the chicken pieces. Add the lettuce, corn, tomato, cabbage and toss well.

Add the avocado, salt, pepper, lemon juice, mayo and toss well.

Serve fresh.

Honey Glazed Chicken Pan Fry with Simple Salad

Pan frying chicken breasts takes less than 10 minutes, but it tastes really good. It complements the baby beetroots and baby cucumbers well.

Serving Size: 1

Cooking Time: 10 Minutes

Ingredients:

- 1 chicken breast
- 1 tsp honey
- Salt and black pepper
- ½ tsp garlic paste
- 1 tbsp butter
- ½ tsp lemon juice
- 1 onion, sliced
- 6 baby beetroots, halved
- 2 baby cucumber, diced
- ½ cup tender arugula
- ½ tsp paprika

Instructions:

Coat the chicken breast in honey, salt, pepper and lemon juice.

Let it marinate for 10 minutes. In a pan melt the butter.

Add the chicken breast and fry until it gets golden. Flip it and again fry till it turns golden.

Transfer to a plate. Combine the beetroot, cucumber, arugula, onion and toss well.

Sprinkle some paprika on top.

Boiled Pasta with Duck and Veggies

Duck requires a little extra time and care to make it tasty. Duck has its own flavors intact so you do not have to use too many spices or sauces to make it delicious. In this dish the duck is accompanied with fresh cucumber and cherry tomatoes and boiled pasta.

Serving Size: 1

Cooking Time: 30 Minutes

Ingredients:

- 1 cup pasta
- 1 duck breast
- 1 tbsp BBQ sauce
- 6 cherry tomatoes, halved
- Salt and pepper to taste
- 1 cucumber, sliced
- 2 lettuce leaves
- 1 tbsp lemon juice
- 1 tbsp honey
- 1 tbsp olive oil
- 1 tsp black sesame seeds

Instructions:

Coat the duck breast in BBQ sauce.

In a pan add the oil and fry the duck breast for 4 minutes. Sprinkle some salt and pepper.

Flip it and fry for 4 minutes. Take off the heat. let it rest. When it has cooled down slightly, slice it into thin pieces.

Combine the lettuce, cherry tomatoes and cucumber. Add lemon juice, salt and pepper and toss well.

In a pot boil the pasta with salted water for 8 minutes. Drain well.

Sprinkle some pepper and black sesame seeds on top.

Assemble everything and serve.

Roasted Sweet Potato Kale and Chickpeas

Have you ever tried roasted sweet potato with chickpeas and kale? Add a gallop of yogurt on top. It will mesmerize you.

Serving Size: 1

Cooking Time: 20 Minutes

Ingredients:

- ½ cup boiled chickpeas
- ½ cup kale, chopped
- ½ cup diced sweet potatoes
- Salt and pepper to taste
- 1 cup yogurt
- ½ tsp paprika
- 1 tsp dried rosemary
- 1 tsp dried oregano

Instructions:

Preheat the oven to 400 degrees F.

Add aluminum foil on a baking tray.

Add the chickpeas, sweet potato and kale on the baking tray.

Sprinkle some salt and pepper, rosemary, oregano and paprika on top.

Bake in the oven for 20 minutes.

Let it rest for 10 minutes. Add to a bowl.

Add the yogurt on top before serving.

Cauliflower Risotto with Fried Scallops

Risotto is a comfort food and no matter what you use in it, veggies or meat, or seafood, it turns out great. This one is with cauliflower instead of rice.

Serving Size: 1

Cooking Time: 20 Minutes

Ingredients:

- 6 scallops, cleaned
- 2 onion, chopped
- 5-6 red chilies
- 1 tbsp chopped parsley
- 1 cup cauliflower floret
- Salt and white pepper to taste
- 2 tbsp butter
- 1 cup vegetable stock
- 1 tsp soy sauce
- 1 tbsp lemon juice

Instructions:

In a pan add half the oil. Add the scallops and fry until they get golden from both sides. Sprinkle some salt and pepper on top. Take off the heat.

In a blender, add the cauliflower and blend for 1 minute.

In a wok, add the rest of the butter.

Add the onion and fry for 1 minute.

Add the cauliflower, salt, pepper, soy sauce and stir well.

Add the stock and bring it to boil. Simmer for 5 minutes.

Add the red chilies, lemon juice and fried scallops on top before serving.

Sesame Chicken with Butter tossed Broccoli and Sticky Rice

This prep may seem overwhelming in the beginning as you have to prepare three different things and all of them require cooking time. But the good news is, it is a complete meal and it will keep you energized for a long time. You can make a big batch and store to eat later in the week.

Serving Size: 1

Cooking Time: 30 Minutes

Ingredients:

- 1 chicken breast
- 1 cup sticky rice
- 1 cup broccoli
- 2 tbsp butter
- 1 tbsp olive oil
- 1 tsp sesame seed (both black and white)
- Salt and pepper to taste
- ½ tsp cumin seeds
- 1 tsp paprika
- 1 tbsp honey
- 1 tsp lemon juice
- ½ tsp garlic paste
- ½ tsp rosemary

Instructions:

To make the sticky rice, in a pan add the butter, cumin seeds and the rice.

Stir them for 3 minutes.

Pour 2 cup of water and cook on high heat until the water evaporates. Fluff the rice with fork.

To make the chicken, marinate it with lemon juice, honey, salt, pepper, garlic paste and rosemary.

Add the oil in the pan and add the chicken. Cook until both sides get golden, it may take 5 minutes per side.

To make the broccoli, add the remaining butter and add the broccoli.

Add salt, pepper, paprika and cook for 5 minutes.

Assemble everything and serve hot.

Chicken Cheesy Sub Sandwich

If you have left over meat in your house then toss them up and come up with a delicious and quick lunch dish. I have used collard leaves here but you can use lettuce or arugula too.

Serving Size: 1

Cooking Time: 5 Minutes

Ingredients:

- 1 sub bun
- 4 collard leaves
- 4 thin slices of cheddar cheese
- 1 /2 cup left-over chicken, thinly sliced
- 1 tbsp ketchup
- Salt and pepper to taste

Instructions:

Toast the sub buns for 2 minutes in the oven or in the pan.

Spread the ketchup onto the buns.

Add collard leaves, chicken pieces, cheese.

Heat it up for 2 minutes in the microwave oven.

Serve hot.

Simple Vegan Sandwich

If you are a vegan or trying vegetarian food for lunch, this sandwich can serve you well. It will be ready in only 5 minutes.

Serving Size: 1

Cooking Time: 5 Minutes

Ingredients:

- 2 brown bread slices
- 2 tomatoes, chopped
- 2 lettuce leaves
- 1 lemon wedge
- Fresh parsley, chopped
- ½ cup avocado puree
- Salt and black pepper to taste
- ¼ tsp chili flakes
- 1 tsp butter
- ¼ tsp rosemary, minced

Instructions:

Toast the bread slices in a grilling pan with butter

Spread the avocado puree generously on both bread slices.

Add the chopped tomatoes, parsley, rosemary, salt, pepper, chili flakes, and the lettuce in the middle.

Serve with the lemon wedge.

Quinoa Salmon Veggie Salad

This is a great salad with many features to it with seared salmon, cabbage, cherry tomatoes and spicy quinoa.

Serving Size: 1

Cooking Time: 20 Minutes

Ingredients:

- ½ cup quinoa
- 1 salmon fillet
- 6 cherry tomatoes
- 1/3 cup arugula
- ¼ cup diced cabbage
- 1 tbsp apple cider vinegar
- Salt and black pepper to taste
- 1 tsp butter
- 1 tsp olive oil
- ½ cup fish stock
- ¼ tsp oregano
- ¼ tsp rosemary

Instructions:

Cook the quinoa with butter, fish stock, oregano, salt and pepper.

It may take about 10 minutes. Fluff it with fork.

Transfer to a bowl.

Fry the salmon with salt, pepper, rosemary in olive oil.

It may take 2 minutes per side. Let it rest for 5 minutes. Cut it into cubes.

Add the vegetables, salmon cubes in the bowl.

Add apple cider vinegar, and toss everything gently.

Serve.

Croquette Wrap

Have you ever eaten croutons wrap before? If you did not, it's time to make yourself some croquette wrap and see how delicious it is.

Serving Size: 1

Cooking Time: 10 Minutes

Ingredients:

- 1 tortilla
- 1 red onion, sliced
- 4 cherry tomatoes, halved
- 2 lettuce leaves, chopped
- 1 jalapeno pepper, chopped
- ¼ tsp lemon juice
- 2 tbsp mayo
- 1 tsp ketchup
- ½ cup minced chicken
- 1 egg
- Salt and pepper to taste
- 1 tsp corn starch
- 2 tbsp olive oil

Instructions:

Combine the minced chicken, egg, salt, pepper, corn starch and mix well. Create little croutons using it.

Fry them golden brown with oil.

Heat the tortilla for 1 minute per side.

Add the onion, lettuce, jalapeno and cherry tomatoes on the tortilla.

Add the ketchup, lemon juice and mayo. Add the fried croquettes.

Wrap it tightly and seal with a toothpick. Enjoy.

Brown Rice with Yogurt Chicken

If you enjoy curries, then this will be the perfect lunch for you. Asians cannot live without rice and this yogurt chicken is perfect to go with the brown rice.

Serving Size: 1

Cooking Time: 30 Minutes

Ingredients:

- 1 cup brown rice
- 2 chicken breasts cut into small pieces
- 1 tsp ginger paste
- 1 tsp garlic paste
- 1 white onion, chopped
- 1 tsp cumin
- ½ tsp turmeric
- ½ cup yogurt
- 1 cinnamon
- 2 tbsp oil
- 1 cardamom
- 1 cup chicken stock
- Chopped coriander to serve
- 2 cup water
- Salt to taste
- 1 tsp red chili powder

Instructions:

Marinate the chicken with yogurt, ginger, garlic, salt, red chili powder, cumin, turmeric and let it sit for 30 minutes.

In a pot add the oil and the onion. Toss for 2 minutes.

Add the cardamom, cinnamon and the chicken mix.

Cover and cook for 10 minutes.

Wait until it becomes thick and take off the heat.

To cook the brown rice, in a pot boil water with 1 pinch of salt.

Add the rice and cook until it becomes tender. It may take about 15 minutes.

Fluff the rice with fork. Serve with the chicken. Add coriander leaves on top.

Pan Fried Crispy Cod with Veggies

If you enjoy eating fish then you would love this recipe. It also contains some veggies that are butter tossed and flavored with herbs and spices.

Serving Size: 1

Cooking Time: 10 Minutes

Ingredients:

- 1 cod fillet, deboned
- 1 potato, cubed
- 1 red bell pepper, cut into stick
- 1 yellow bell pepper, cut into stick
- 1 green bell pepper, cut into stick
- Salt to taste
- 1 tbsp butter
- ½ tsp rosemary
- 1/3 tsp cumin
- 1 tsp chopped parsley
- 1 tbsp oil
- 1 tbsp corn starch
- Black pepper to taste

Instructions:

Combine the corn starch, salt, pepper, rosemary and mix well. Add a drop of water to make a paste.

Coat the cod fish in it and shallow fry it golden brown in oil.

Transfer to a plate. In another pan melt the butter.

Add the potatoes and sprinkle some salt, pepper, cumin and toss for 5 minutes.

Add the bell peppers and toss for 2 minutes. Add the parsley and serve with the fish.

Turkey Avocado Lettuce Goat Cheese Salad

This is a powerhouse of nutrition and it also tastes quite good. If you can't find turkey, you can use duck or chicken here. You can use regular cheese instead of goat cheese too.

Serving Size: 1

Cooking Time: 10 Minutes

Ingredients:

- ½ turkey breast
- 1 cup chopped lettuce
- 8 walnuts, toasted, chopped
- Salt and pepper to taste
- 2 tbsp lemon juice
- 1 tbsp butter
- 1 avocado, cubed
- 4 cherry tomatoes, chopped
- Fresh parsley, chopped
- 1 tsp garlic powder
- 1 tsp honey

Instructions:

Marinate the turkey breast using honey, salt, pepper, and garlic powder.

In a pan melt the butter and fry the turkey breast for 5 minutes on each side.

Let it rest for 10 minutes. Chop it finely.

In a mixing bowl combine the turkey cubes with all the veggies.

Add lemon juice, parsley, salt, pepper, and walnut.

Toss well and serve.

Minced Chicken Red Beans Tomato Curry with Cabbage and Avocado

This tastes as good as it looks. It is best to serve it with semi ripe avocado slices and shredded cabbage on the side. One squeeze of lemon increases the flavors.

Serving Size: 1

Cooking Time: 20 Minutes

Ingredients:

- 1 cup minced chicken
- ½ cup tomato puree
- ½ cup boiled red beans
- 1 cup chicken stock
- 1 tsp cumin
- ½ tsp red chili powder
- ¼ tsp oregano
- 1 tsp garlic powder
- 1 tsp oil
- Salt and pepper to taste
- 2 lemon wedges to serve
- 1 avocado, sliced, to serve
- ½ cup shredded cabbage, to serve

Instructions:

In a pan, add the oil and toss the chicken for 3 minutes.

Add the red beans, garlic powder, cumin and red chili powder.

Toss for 2 minutes and add the tomato puree.

Cook for 2 minutes and pour in the stock.

Cook on high heat for 5 minutes.

Add the salt, pepper, oregano and cook for 2 minutes.

Serve with avocado, cabbage and lemon wedges.

Chickpea Croutons Avocado Baby Cabbage Salad

When you add croutons to your salad, no matter how little ingredients the salad contains, the final result tastes great. Try to pick ripe avocado to make this salad.

Serving Size: 1

Cooking Time: 5 Minutes

Ingredients:

- 1 cup boiled chickpeas
- 2 bread slices
- 1 tbsp butter
- 1 ripe avocado, sliced
- 1 red onion, chopped
- ½ cup baby cabbage, chopped
- 1 tomato, chopped
- Fresh parsley, chopped
- Salt and pepper to taste
- 1 tbsp apple cider vinegar

Instructions:

In a pan add the butter. Fry the bread until they become crispy and golden in color.

Transfer to a plate, cut it into thin small cubes.

In a mixing bowl combine the cabbage, avocado, tomato, onion, parsley, and chickpeas.

Add salt, pepper, and vinegar. Toss well and finally add the croutons.

Serve immediately.

Quinoa Chickpea Blueberry and Veggie Salad

Quinoa

This is such an extraordinary salad that it deserves a special day to eat it. Only when you are feeling very happy and to treat yourself, you should make this unique and delicious salad.

Serving Size: 1

Cooking Time: 10 Minutes

Ingredients:

- ½ cup quinoa
- ½ cup spinach leaves
- 1/3 cup boiled chickpeas
- 1 tomato, chopped
- 1/3 cup blueberries
- 2 tbsp goat cheese, torn
- 1 ripe avocado, sliced
- Fresh mint leaves
- 1/3 tsp chia seeds
- Salt and pepper to taste
- 1 tbsp toasted pecans

Instructions:

Cook the quinoa in butter and water for 10 minutes.

Fluff it with a fork and add to a mixing bowl.

Add the avocado, spinach, tomato, blueberry, and chickpeas.

Toss well and add the salt, pepper, cheese, chia seeds, and toss one more time.

Serve.

Fish with Green Beans Cherry Tomato and Olives

This is a simple fish and stir fry veggie recipe which is highly nutritious. Feel free add or omit the veggies in the recipe.

Serving Size: 1

Cooking Time: 6 Minutes

Ingredients:

- 2 salmon fillets, deboned
- Salt to taste
- Black pepper to taste
- 2 tbsp butter
- ½ cup baby green beans
- ½ cup baby cherry tomatoes
- 4 black olives, pitted
- 1 tsp chopped rosemary

Instructions:

In a pan add half the butter.

Add the fish and sprinkle salt, pepper and add the rosemary.

Cook for 3 minutes on each side. Transfer to your serving plate.

In the same pan add 1 tbsp butter and toss the green beans for 1 minute.

Add the cherry tomatoes and toss for 1 minute.

Add the olives, salt, pepper and toss for another minute.

Serve hot.

Conclusion

Working from home may sound easy but in reality the hassle is even harder. You do not have as much distractions in the office as you may face at home. You also aim at getting the work done on time so the hassle is double when you work from home. It is important to keep you energetic. You have to be productive throughout your working hours. To ensure good productivity during your work hours, you need to eat a balanced lunch. Try these recipes and see which ones are more convenient to make on a daily basis.

About the Author

Born in New Germantown, Pennsylvania, Stephanie Sharp received a Masters degree from Penn State in English Literature. Driven by her passion to create culinary masterpieces, she applied and was accepted to The International Culinary School of the Art Institute where she excelled in French cuisine. She has married her cooking skills with an aptitude for business by opening her own small cooking school where she teaches students of all ages.

Stephanie's talents extend to being an author as well and she has written over 400 e-books on the art of cooking and baking that include her most popular recipes.

Sharp has been fortunate enough to raise a family near her hometown in Pennsylvania where she, her husband and children live in a beautiful rustic house on an extensive piece of land. Her other passion is taking care of the furry members of her family which include 3 cats, 2 dogs and a potbelly pig named Wilbur.

Watch for more amazing books by Stephanie Sharp coming out in the next few months.

Author's Afterthoughts

I am truly grateful to you for taking the time to read my book. I cherish all of my readers! Thanks ever so much to each of my cherished readers for investing the time to read this book!

With so many options available to you, your choice to buy my book is an honour, so my heartfelt thanks at reading it from beginning to end!

I value your feedback, so please take a moment to submit an honest and open review on Amazon so I can get valuable insight into my readers' opinions and others can benefit from your experience.

Thank you for taking the time to review!

Stephanie Sharp

For announcements about new releases, please follow my author page on Amazon.com!

You can find that at:

https://www.amazon.com/author/stephanie-sharp

*or Scan **QR-code** below.*